AUG   2011

W9-ALW-190

UH-60 BLACK HAWKS

BY CARLOS ALVAREZ

Are you ready to take it to the extreme?
Torque books thrust you into the action-packed
world of sports, vehicles, and adventure. These books
may include dirt, smoke, fire, and dangerous stunts.
WARNING: read at your own risk.

Library of Congress Cataloging-in-Publication Data

Alvarez, Carlos, 1968-
  UH-60 Black Hawks / by Carlos Alvarez.
    p. cm. — (Torque: military machines)
  Includes bibliographical references and index.
  Summary: "Amazing photography accompanies engaging information about UH-60 Black Hawks.
The combination of high-interest subject matter and light text is intended for students in grades 3
through 7"—Provided by publisher.
  ISBN 978-1-60014-581-0 (hardcover : alk. paper)
  1. Black Hawk (Military transport helicopter)—Juvenile literature. I. Title.
  UG1232.T72A47 2011
  623.74'65—dc22   2010034520

This edition first published in 2011 by Bellwether Media, Inc.

The images in this book are reproduced through the courtesy of: Ted Carlson/Fotodynamics, front cover,
pp. 4-5, 10-11, 16, 17, 18-19, 19 (small), 20-21; all other photos courtesy of the Department of Defense.

Printed in the United States of America, North Mankato, MN.
010111   1176

CONTENTS

THE UH-60 BLACK HAWK IN ACTION

A group of United States Army vehicles rumbles down a rough desert road. Suddenly, the sounds of explosions and gunfire fill the air. It's an **ambush**! The U.S. soldiers are outnumbered by the enemy. They use their radios to call for backup. The Army sends six UH-60 Black Hawk helicopters to help.

UNITED STATES ARMY

425

5

Each Black Hawk carries 11 heavily armed U.S. soldiers. The helicopters open fire as they approach the battle. They land nearby and the soldiers rush out to join the fight. The U.S. soldiers now outnumber the enemy.

In 1979, the U.S. Army replaced the UH-1 Huey with the UH-60 Black Hawk. The Black Hawk took over many of the Huey's roles.

The Black Hawks return to the air. Their guns help the soldiers drive the enemy back. The enemy is forced to **retreat**. The soldiers return to the Black Hawks and head back to base. The Army vehicles continue down the road on their **mission**.

MEDIUM-LIFT UTILITY HELICOPTER

The UH-60 Black Hawk is a medium-lift **utility** helicopter. It has many **variants**. The first variant was the UH-60A. It entered U.S. Army service in 1979 to carry soldiers, heavy weapons, and equipment into battle. The Army later added the UH-60L and UH-60M. These variants have better engines and electronics. The UH-60Q performs medical **evacuations**. The UH-60C is used for command missions. All of the variants are based on the original Black Hawk design.

The Black Hawk has been an
important part of every major U.S. Army
conflict since it entered service in 1979.
It has served in Somalia, Afghanistan,
and both Gulf Wars. It has proven to be
critical to the success of many missions.

★ FAST FACT ★

United States Army Special Forces use the MH-60A and MH-60L variants of the Black Hawk.

WEAPONS AND FEATURES

The Black Hawk needs a lot of power to complete its missions. It has two GE T700 **turboshaft** engines. They give the helicopter the ability to lift up to 9,000 pounds (4,082 kilograms) of **cargo**. The helicopter can keep flying even if one engine is damaged.

15

7.62mm machine gun

The Black Hawk is not heavily armed. It normally carries just two 7.62mm **machine guns**. Some Black Hawks can be fitted with more weapons mounts for attack missions. These mounts can hold missiles, **rockets**, or extra guns.

UH-60L
SPECIFICATIONS:

Primary Function: Medium-lift utility helicopter

Length: 64 feet, 10 inches (19.8 meters)

Height: 16 feet, 10 inches (5.1 meters)

Rotor Diameter: 53 feet, 8 inches
(16.4 meters)

Maximum Weight: 22,000 pounds
(9,979 kilograms)

Top Speed: 184 miles (296 kilometers) per hour

Ceiling: 19,150 feet (5,837 meters)

Range: 504 miles (811 kilometers)

Crew: 3-4

UH-60 MISSIONS

A crew of three or four operates a UH-60 during missions. A pilot and co-pilot fly the Black Hawk. One or two **crew chiefs** are in charge of the weapons. The crew chiefs are also responsible for the helicopter's mechanical systems and cargo. The crew must work together in order for missions to be successful.

★ **FAST FACT** ★

One variant of the Black Hawk, the VH-60N White Hawk, is used to transport the President of the United States.

The Black Hawk is used for many different missions. Its main mission is to transport soldiers. It can carry a full **squad** of 11 soldiers with all of their gear. The UH-60 can also transport other equipment and supplies. It is sometimes sent to assist in combat missions or to rescue wounded soldiers.

The Black Hawk has proven successful in all of these roles. Its many uses make it one of the most important helicopters in the United States Army.

GLOSSARY

ambush—a sudden, surprise attack

cargo—goods carried by a vehicle

crew chiefs—the Black Hawk crew members who are responsible for the helicopter's mechanical systems, cargo, and weapons

evacuations—moving people out of dangerous situations; the UH-60Q is used to evacuate wounded soldiers to receive medical treatment.

machine guns—automatic weapons that rapidly fire bullets

mission—a military task

retreat—to go back to a safer location

rockets—flying explosives that are not guided

squad—the smallest unit of the U.S. Army, usually made up of 9 or 10 soldiers and their commanding officer

turboshaft—a type of engine that produces power by spinning a drive shaft

utility—serving many functions

variants—versions of something; there are many variants of the Black Hawk that do different jobs.

TO LEARN MORE

AT THE LIBRARY

David, Jack. *United States Army*. Minneapolis, Minn.: Bellwether Media, 2008.

Green, Michael. *Weapons Carrier Helicopters: The UH-60 Black Hawks*. Mankato, Minn.: Capstone Press, 2005.

Von Finn, Denny. *Military Helicopters*. Minneapolis, Minn.: Bellwether Media, 2010.

ON THE WEB

Learning more about military machines is as easy as 1, 2, 3.

1. Go to www.factsurfer.com.

2. Enter "military machines" into the search box.

3. Click the "Surf" button and you will see a list of related Web sites.

With factsurfer.com, finding more information is just a click away.

INDEX